Old NEWMAINS
And the villages around Wishaw
by
Lewis Hutton

The coachwork of this car was built by John Stewart's works, located just outside Cambusnethan in Kirk Road, Wishaw.

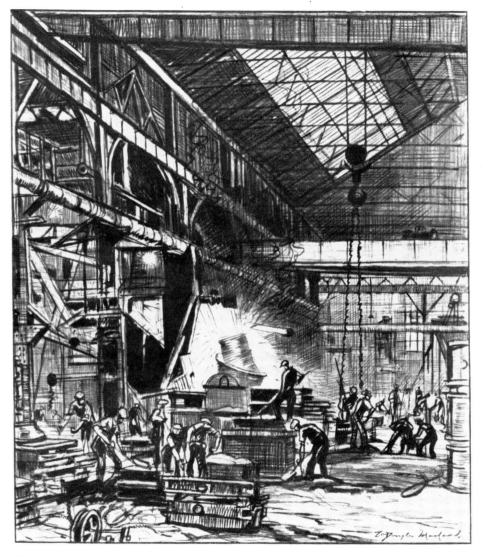

The Coltness Iron Company's steel moulding shop.

© Lewis Hutton 1999
First published in the United Kingdom, 1999,
by Stenlake Publishing, Ochiltree Sawmill, The Lade,
Ochiltree, Ayrshire, KA18 2NX
Telephone / Fax: 01290 423114

ISBN 1 84033 070 8

ACKNOWLEDGEMENT

Thanks to David H. Smith for reading the manuscript
and providing additional information.

THE PUBLISHERS REGRET THAT
THEY CANNOT SUPPLY COPIES OF
ANY PICTURES FEATURED IN THIS BOOK.

INTRODUCTION

To tell the story of the villages surrounding Wishaw is to tell the story of one of the earliest and most successful heavy industrial ventures in Scotland. There were three important iron and steel developments in the area; strung out in a line from west to east they were the Omoa Ironworks, the Coltness Iron Company, and the Shotts Iron Company. Together they represented one of the most important concentrations of iron and steel manufacture in Scotland. This book covers the first two of these works and the area surrounding them.

Dating from 1860, the Carron Ironworks on the Forth was the earliest ironworks to be established in Scotland. No more works were built until the late 1780s and 1790s, but the Omoa Ironworks, established in 1789, was amongst the first of this second wave. Like many early ironworks in Scotland it was established by an Englishman with a Scottish partner, because there was neither the expertise nor the money locally for the venture to be purely Scottish. Using coal mined on Knownoble Hill and in the grounds of Cleland House, the works had an unusual source for supplementing its supply of ironstone, paying local people for what they found in streams and fields in the locality. Several cartloads of ironstone a week were secured by this method, which was effectively stealing from the people who owned the land (and hence the mineral wealth below it).

Fifty years after the establishment of the Omoa works, Henry Houldsworth, another Englishman, approached the Steuarts of Coltness with a view to buying their estate to develop the mineral wealth below it. To the Steuarts it was just an upland estate, windswept and of limited farming potential, so they sold it. It is perhaps debatable whether they would have done so if they had known just how valuable the underground resources were, and the scale of the enterprise that Henry Houldsworth would build there. The early years of the Coltness Iron Company, from its establishment in 1837 until the railway reached it four years later, were nonetheless very lean. But using coal and iron ore mined from the Coltness Estate, the company grew into one of the most important iron and steel manufacturers in Scotland. It also developed

the clays of the estate and operated brick and tile works at a number of locations and a cement works in Newmains.

Towards the end of the nineteenth century better quality ore won from mines in Spain and Cumbria was imported in preference to ironstone from Scottish ironfields. This corresponded with a decline in the importance of iron-making to the Coltness Iron Company, but despite this it still exploited Scottish coal, and coal mining became the mainstay of the company's activities after 1890. It operated numerous mines in Lanarkshire, Ayrshire, Fife, the Lothians, and also in Cumbria. By the time that Britain's coal and iron industries were nationalised, the Coltness Iron Company had made the name of Newmains famous throughout the world.

The Coltness Iron Company dominated the economy of much of the area covered by this book, and from its headquarters at Newmains it spread out to encompass the small communities of Cambusnethan, Morningside, Waterloo and Overtown. It changed the character of those villages from an agrarian to a mining-based one, and provided the impetus for the growth and development of their communities. As coal was exhausted, the company had to look further afield for new reserves, founding an industrial colony at Allanton where it exploited the hidden coalfield.

The first settlement associated with the Omoa Ironworks was the village of Omoa itself, built for those who were employed in the works. This failed to survive the demise of the ironworks, and all that is left is the name, which confusingly still appears in several locations across the local area. Cleland grew adjacent to the Omoa works, providing accommodation and services for the miners that worked the coal and ironstone mines surrounding the works. More substantial than the village of Omoa that it superseded, Cleland survived the closure of the works and still exists today.

Lewis Hutton, June 1999

CLELAND HOUSE.

Cleland House lay just to the west of Cleland, on the site now occupied by the Dalzell Golf Club. For many years the grounds of the house were mined for coal to supply the nearby Omoa Ironworks. Below the house on the banks of the Calder is a cave reputed to have been used as a hiding place by William Wallace when he was being pursued by the English; the cave was more certainly used by Covenanters hiding from persecution. In 1900 Cleland House was bought by the MP John Colville, the owner of the Dalzell Steelworks in Motherwell, shortly before his early death. During his occupancy it became one of the principle centres of the temperance workers in the area.

OMOA SQUARE

Omoa Square stood on the north side of Omoa Road, immediately to the east of the Tillan Burn, and was originally built to house the workers of the Omoa Ironworks that lay south of the road. The ironworks was one of the earliest in Scotland, built in 1789 by William Waller of Chesterfield and his Scottish partner Colonel William Dalrymple. The village and works were named after the battle at which Colonel Dalrymple had distinguished himself, capturing the fort of San Fernando de Omoa and town of Omoa in Honduras in 1779. The ironworks closed in 1868, two years after the death of the penultimate owner, Robert Stewart of Murdostoun.

Omoa Road was once the main street of Cleland, and the original line of the village ran east/west along it. The Omoa Ironworks, the focus for Cleland's early development, lay at the western end of the road. When the station on the Caledonian Railway's main Glasgow to Edinburgh line was built the village reorientated itself, with Main Street being built on a north/south alignment to meet it.

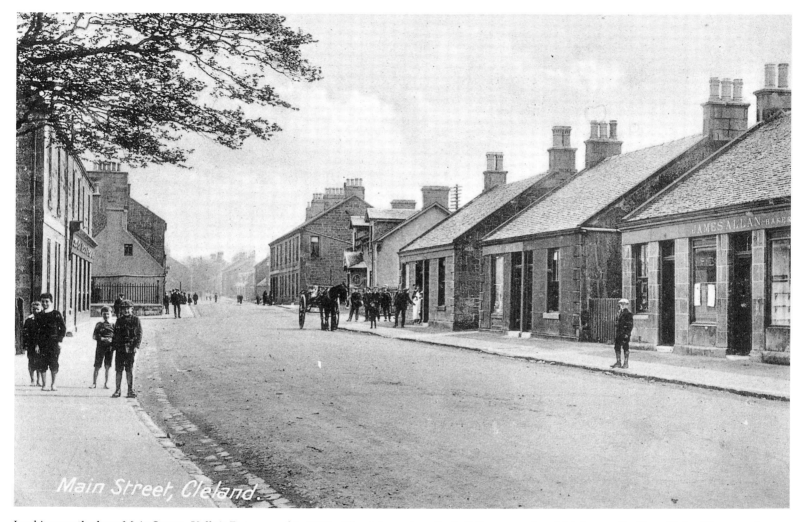

Main Street, Cleland.

Looking north along Main Street. Kelly's Bar, opened in 1880, still exists, as does the building opposite which is now the Cross Cafe. We can no longer sample the delights of James Allan's bakery as it and the other shops on the right have become houses. The opening on the right hand side of the street, in front of the building with dormer windows, leads into Station Road. Cleland station, on the line from Holytown to Morningside, closed to passengers on 1 December 1930.

Main Street, Cleland. Very little of the original street remains, with the post office building one of the few landmarks to give the viewer any clue to the location. The library now occupies the site of the co-op on the near right hand side.

Looking north along Main Street from the cross, Cleland. As with the previous picture most of the buildings have gone, victims of a phase of road widening. New shops now stand on the left.

OMOA HOUSE.

Omoa House was built as a combination poorhouse (so-called because a number of parishes banded together to establish it) by the parishes of Shotts, Bothwell and Cambusnethan. It was originally planned to accommodate 186 inmates, but on completion the respective parishes felt that the architect had been too lenient, and decided it could house 258 people instead. Unlike most combination poorhouses Omoa House did not keep mentally ill patients; it transferred them to the Hartwood Asylum. The building is now used by the Lanarkshire NHS Trust as Cleland Hospital. This photograph was taken shortly after Omoa House opened in 1903.

County Gardens, Cleland

Fraser Street was one of a number of streets built in the Knownoble area of Cleland during the 1920s to provide housing for miners and their families who were moved out of their cramped rows into these better-appointed houses. Gardens were provided to allow some room to grow vegetables.

Aldersyde (now Parkside), to the north of the railway, is a very fine terrace of houses, which, along with the rows further up the hill, was built to house the workers of the nearby Omoa Iron Foundry (later the Omoa Boiler Works). They replaced the rows of Omoa Square on the other side of the railway, which were demolished soon after these houses were built.

The old station building on the Caledonian Railway's Edinburgh and Glasgow line. The station was initially known as Bellside, but the name was changed to Omoa in 1879. It underwent a second change of name in 1941 when it became Cleland station (the former Cleland station having closed some years previously). The station was badly damaged in 1912 when it dropped four feet after a collapse of mine workings underneath it. The workings were probably those of the Howmuir Colliery which lay just to the north of the station in the 1850s.

This viaduct was an important feature on the Caledonian Railway's Edinburgh and Glasgow line. The opening of the line in 1869 allowed the Caledonian to challenge the North British Railway's dominance of freight and passenger traffic between the two cities. With the opening of the new line a vicious price-war began. In addition to trying to undercut each other's fares, the two companies ran 54 trains a day between them, many of them nearly empty. Once the competition had settled down the Caledonian ran ten stopping trains and five expresses on its line each day; the expresses took a speedy 65 minutes between the two cities.

Nestling in the lee of the viaduct and adjacent to the former poorhouse is the settlement of Bellside, a pleasant collection of buildings in the wooded glade. Cleland Parish Church can be seen in the distance. Situated in what seems an idyllic rural location, it is in fact only minutes from the busy cross and Main Street of Cleland. The tranquillity is even more deceptive than it initially appears; the piggery and sawmill of Omoa House also occupied this glade, together with the Bellside Quarry to the north side of the railway.

The tower of Cambusnethan Old Parish Church can be seen above the church halls in this view along Greenhead Road. The entrance to the graveyard is to the right. The church was begun in 1839, but owing to a dispute between the Reverend Archibald Livingstone and the presbytery over the fees paid for the reading of banns it was not completed until 1857.

Looking across Walter Street towards Wishaw from the tower of Cambusnethan Old Parish Church. Note the haystacks in the field to the middle left; a sight unlikely to be seen in today's Cambusnethan. In the background, behind the wall, is Houldsworth Park, given to Wishaw by the family of the same name.

Again taken from the Old Parish Church tower, this picture looks towards Cambusnethan past the remains of the former Cambusnethan church, and the North Church. The North Church, built in 1903, owes its existence to the Disruption of 1843 when a breakaway congregation following the Free Church formed in Cambusnethan.

The west end of Cambusnethan with the tower of the Old Parish Church on the skyline. 'The Auld Hoose' and the Masonic Lodge are other landmarks still in existence. The memorial stone of the lodge house was laid in 1904 by Colonel Robert King Stewart, owner of Murdostoun Castle, and son of the former owner of the Omoa Ironworks. Colonel Stewart was one of the most prominent members of the Masonic brotherhood in Scotland, and held the post of Substitute Grand Master Mason.

This stretch of Cambusnethan Street was formerly called Anderson Street. Establishing a water supply was a problem in Cambusnethan – as the village was sited on top of a hill, the main source came from rain which villagers collected in barrels. In 1859 Cambusnethan secured a more permanent source when water began to be pumped from the disused Thrashbush ironstone mine, just behind the primary school. This was supplied to a number of standpipes in the streets of the village. Perhaps the most bitter irony is that whilst he was Lord Provost of Glasgow, Colonel Stewart's father had been instrumental in providing the city with a supply from Loch Katrine, described as 'the envy of the inhabitants of other municipalities in the kingdom', while Cambusnethan had to make do with brackish old mine water.

A meeting of carts in Cambusnethan Street. Cambusnethan was originally a weaving village with nearly all the inhabitants employed in domestic weaving. It was fortunate that the decline of the industry in the 1840s was mitigated by the growth of coal and steel working in the area. Within ten years Cambusnethan was transformed from an ailing weaving community to a vibrant industrial colony of the Coltness Iron Company, which employed over 100 pitmen and 90 ironworkers from the village.

Cambusnethan Street, this time looking toward Newmains; the building with the lantern fixed to it is the Horse and Anchor. The stacks and buildings of the Coltness Iron Company's works, founded in 1837, dominate the skyline. The company was established to exploit the mineral resources of the Coltness Estate, thought to have 2,000 acres of workable reserves yielding 18,000 tons of coal and 1,000 tons of ironstone per acre. The riches of the estate allowed the enterprise to grow to become one of the largest in Scotland. On the right hand side, in the middle distance by the single storey cottages, is the entrance to Moss Road, which led to Cambusnethan station. The station was closed on 1 January 1917 as an economy measure and never reopened.

Looking up Manse Road towards Cambusnethan along the tramlines that once connected Newmains with Cambuslang. From there Lanarkshire Tramways Co. lines connected with Glasgow Corporation trams, but there was never a through service to Glasgow and a change of 'caur' was necessary to complete the journey to the city. To the left is the striking facade of the Coltness Memorial Church Halls, with the tower of the church visible behind the halls. A row of shops now stands on the right instead of the trees seen here. The railway line that can just be seen crossing the road in the distance would have cut through the shops where the Chinese restaurant is now.

A Newmains to Cambuslang tram, photographed outside what is now 507 Cambusnethan Street (to the left). Trams first reached Newmains and Cambusnethan on 29 June 1909, six years after the construction of a tramway was authorised by the Lanarkshire Tramways Order of 1903. Trams ran on the route until 6 October 1930, when the last car, travelling at midnight, marked the termination of the service. The date of closure had originally been set for the previous week, but the trams won a reprieve for seven days after it was pointed out how much chaos this would cause on Saturday 4 October. Motherwell were playing a home game against Clyde at Fir Park, and the tram was a vital part of the passenger link to the game.

No. 103 Manse Road, Newmains

Looking towards the cross past the location of the Spar store, which was once a co-op shop. The workers' row on the right has been replaced by the health centre and library. Stores to feed and clothe the communities that supplied their workers were initially provided and operated by the Coltness Iron Company, but as soon as they found suitable tenants such stores were passed to them. Supplying goods to the citizens of the village then became the responsibility of the store-keeper, who had to give a pledge not to sell intoxicants. The first shop-owner in Newmains was John Kirkland who in 1860 leased the village store from the company for the sum of £600 a year. Kirkland was able to make a very profitable living for himself and subsequently used his profits to become one of the main property owners in Wishaw.

Taken from Westwood Road and looking towards Manse Road, this is a very early picture of the cross at Newmains. The future site of the police station (built in 1916) can be seen facing the camera. Gas was introduced to Newmains in the 1840s in an attempt by the Coltness Iron Company to encourage their workers to adopt a more family-orientated lifestyle. They thought that the better light it provided would encourage reading and staying at home, as opposed to a life of disreputable pursuits out of doors and in public houses.

THE CROSS, MAIN STREET, NEWMAINS.

B.6089.

Looking up Main Street from the cross and war memorial. All the buildings in this photograph have now been demolished leaving the memorial standing on its own traffic island. It is plain to see that a sickening number of local men died during the First World War, with the visible side of the memorial covered by their names. More than 400 Coltness Iron Company employees joined up in the first week of the war, and that number steadily mounted. By the end of 1914 nearly 700 men had left the pits, and production costs began to rise sharply. This didn't stop the company from providing the wives of those miners who had joined up with a monthly allowance of coal and the right to stay in their houses rent free.

No. 101 Main Street, Newmains

Main Street was part of the main road between Ayr and Edinburgh, and the original focus of the village of Newmains. Now all that remains of the street are the name plates on the police station. In the early years of the Coltness Iron Company's existence, the village was too small to supply all its employment needs and skilled labour had to be imported, hastening Newmains' growth. As a consequence of this need to import labour, the iron company paid its workers more than many of its competitors, something that was an early source of criticism of the company.

Looking north from a chimney of the Coltness Iron Company. The building at the bottom left housed the company's mineral offices; nestling behind them in the trees can be seen Newmains House. Most of the other buildings have been lost in the widening of Main Street. Just below the horizon on the right is the rectangle of the bowling green; beyond that are the streets of Cambusnethan.

Looking across the workers' rows that have made way for a widened Main Street are the landmarks of the Memorial Church and the old school building. The railway running behind the school (which crosses Manse Road in the middle distance) connected the company's works with the pits at Branchal, to the north-west of Newmains. The road running away from the camera is School Road.

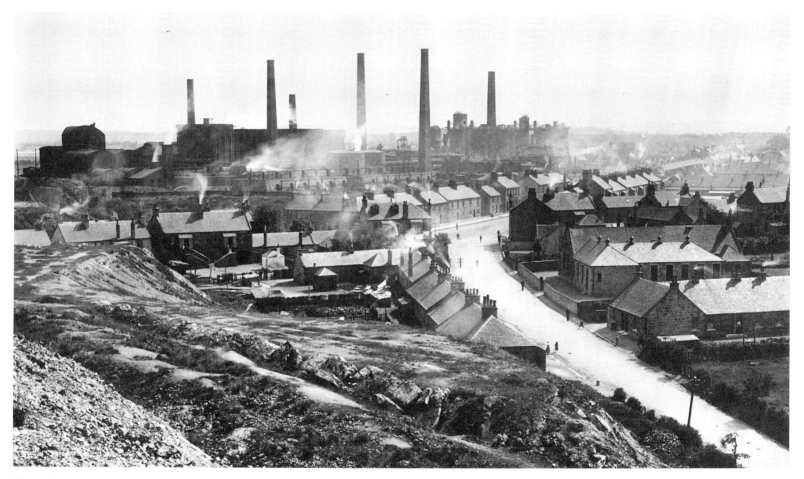

The Coltness Iron Company's works dominated Newmains and provided the impetus for the small estate village to grow into a town. This picture of the works, framed by the smoke and grime that attended the success of industrial enterprise, was taken from a waste bing. Despite the pollution, the works brought glory to the town, producing some of the castings for the Forth Rail Bridge; bomb casings for the RAF and Russian air force during World War II; and locomotive turbine framings of the finest steel.

Looking over the workers' rows of Westwood Road, with Eastwood Drive leading off to the right in the foreground. The predominantly agricultural scenery contrasts starkly with the heavy industry of the previous photograph, yet this picture was taken a from similar spot on the waste bing, but looking in the opposite direction. The difference in the two views could hardly be more pronounced.

This school was built to replace the old school building in 1906 after parishes became responsible for the provision of schooling facilities. The earlier school, now the nursery school and visible in the panorama of Newmains on the right of page 28, was built by the Coltness Iron Company. They deducted two old pence from each employee's wage packet every week to help pay for the building, staffing and management of schools. The company built five of these in villages where their workers lived, long before the Education Act of 1872 required them to provide schools.

Newmains House, just visible in the leftmost panorama of Newmains on page 28, was a grand building that once stood across from the mineral offices of the Coltness Iron Company. It was built for James Hunter, one of the partners, a man who concerned himself greatly with the quality of the work carried out by the company. Whenever he was in residence at Newmains he toured the works at least once a day to monitor the employees. The house was later demolished to make way for the Stonecraigs No. 5 pit. That is exactly what James Hunter would have wanted; he hated to see anything go to waste, and if there was coal under the house it would have to be demolished so that the coal could be removed.

Bowling Green & Coltness Memorial Church Newmains

The Coltness Memorial Church was built in 1878 and is dedicated to the memory of James Houldsworth's eldest son, who died at school at the age of 11 (Houldsworth was a partner in the Coltness Iron Company). In the foreground is the bowling green, laid out by the company in 1892. The Coltness company was keen to encourage leisure activities amongst its workers and attempted to give them more free time than other companies. As well as the bowling green it provided the football fields at Victoria Park and indoor sports facilities in the Gospel Hall.

The clubhouse of 1929, which has since made way for a more modern structure, was built to replace the much smaller building that can be seen in the panorama from the chimney of the works. It is seen here at its opening on 7 September 1929, with a wide section of the community of Newmains present.

THE CROSS, LOOKING UP BONKLE ROAD, NEWMAINS.   B.6094.

Looking up Bonkle Road towards the cross. The gable end of the building on the right carries a quaint advertisement for Butlin's in Ayr. This building has now been demolished and the site is occupied by the touching memorial to the boxer Jim Murray, who died after collapsing in the ring on 13 October 1995.

Crindledyke Road, Newmains

314

Looking down Bonkle Road from the edge of one of the spoil bings. The bridge in the foreground crosses the railway line that once served Newmains; the station was located just behind the crest of the bing on the left. The road to the station can be seen on the other side of the bridge.

"GOING TO SEE THE KING" NEWMAINS N°1

King George V visited Lanarkshire in 1914 during his first royal visit to Scotland. On 9 July he passed through Newmains at 1.37, on his way to a late lunch at Mauldslie Castle near Carluke. I wonder how many of those who turned out to meet the king gave a thought to his relative Archduke Ferdinand of Austria, who had been buried a few days earlier.

Morningside, with the shops and businesses that once supplied the inhabitants of the mining village on the left. The Coltness Iron Company, who employed most of the workers here, ran an extremely paternalistic regime with strict management supervision both above and below ground. This paternalistic approach may have been one of the reasons why the union failed to make inroads amongst the workers of the Coltness company in the early years. During a Lanarkshire miners' strike in 1863 the Morningside and Chapel miners did, however, show solidarity with their fellow miners by donating £10 of their wages to the relief of the striking miners' families.

St Columba's Church, Morningside. The mineral station of the Caledonian Railway Company is in the background; the station of its rival in Lanarkshire, the North British Railway, stood on the opposite side of the road. Unfortunately for the North British they owned no turntable at Morningside, and had to rely on the goodwill of the Caledonian to turn their engines around. This was a privilege that was sometimes refused, forcing them to run trains tender-first down the steep grades to their station. Both companies also had passenger stations in Morningside.

Murdostoun Castle, Wishaw.

The present Murdostoun Castle is a fairly recent structure, grafted onto the vaults of a building thought to be several hundred years old. It was owned by Robert Stewart, Lord Provost of Glasgow (who also owned the Omoa Ironworks), and later by his son Colonel Robert King Stewart. Murdostoun was much noted for being the first large residence in the area to be lit by electric light. It is now a nursing home and brain injury rehabilitation unit run by the Scotcare Group Ltd.

CHURCH STREET, BONKLE, NEWMAINS.

B.6090.

Bonkle lies just off the eastern edge of the mineral field that supplied Newmains with the wealth needed to grow its industry. To the west the coals are generally within 100 to 200 metres of the surface; they are at the considerably greater depth of 400 metres below the village of Bonkle, and lie in a concealed field with no clues on the surface that the coal is below. As a result of these factors the settlement never grew beyond its role as an estate village in the lee of Murdostoun Castle.

Allanton, Shotts.

Allanton lies above the same mineral field as Bonkle, and was built between the wars to house miners from Kingshill Colliery working that field. The first shaft, which became Kingshill No. 1, was begun by the Coltness Iron Company in 1914 and completed in 1918. It is interesting to note that the bell on Calderhead Parish church is a later addition, and had yet to be added at the time this photograph was taken.

Waterloo, looking down the Carluke and Lanark road. Like many other Waterloos in Britain, the village was built to house veterans of that battle. This particular Waterloo was built by the last of the Steuarts of Coltness, Sir James, who it is said also planted strips of woodland around the village to represent opposing armies at the battle.

Overtown, south of Waterloo, seen from the railway bridge. The old stone bridge has now been replaced by a more modern concrete one. Overtown was another village transformed by the coal industry. In the 1840s most of the population was involved in farming and fruit growing in the many nearby farms and orchards, but in the 1850s and 1860s several colliery developments around the village – at Overtown, Gowkthrapple, and the Garriongill collieries – completely transformed the nature of the local economy.

Looking northward along Main Street from the shop-front of what was once G. Barr's the bootmakers, and the Railway Inn. The railway was the Wishaw and Coltness Railway, which passed just to the north of Overtown on its way south from Whifflet, near Coatbridge, through Wishaw to Morningside and to the works at Newmains. It was one of the earliest in Scotland, initially authorised for construction in 1829.

Main Street, this time looking south, with the Railway Inn on the right and the spire of the church just visible on the skyline. Built in the 1850s by a coal company that had long since left the area, the quality of miners' housing in Overtown was for many years considered to be dreadful. The majority of the houses consisted of a single room; none of them had running water or sinks; and drainage was open to the air outside the buildings. In the 1870s the Coltness company began building rows in Overtown, most of which were two apartment dwellings, a few having a third room. Whilst these were an improvement on the previous dwellings they were still damp; only houses built after 1900 were constructed according to new regulations which required a damp course in the walls.

Overtown, Wishaw.

This picture was taken from the vicinity of the church looking south out of Overtown, where the road drops steeply down into the Clyde Valley. Mining communities are often noted for their bands, and Newmains silver band had a formidable reputation. Not to be outdone, Overtown miners formed their own (brass) band in 1884, and then went a step further by forming a string band as well a few years later. Neither of these diminished the level of home-made musical entertainment, with the sound of melodeon, concertina and fiddle commonly coming from amongst the rows.

Miners Institute, Overtown

Finlayson Photo

The bands of Overtown presumably played a key part in the concert held to celebrate the opening of the Overtown Miners' Institute in 1924. The institute was a valuable local amenity, containing a hall seating 500 people, a projection box, cloakrooms, kitchen, billiard room, reading room, and private baths and showers. It was demolished a few years ago due to structural deterioration.